We All Share

FAMILY
AROUND THE WORLD

BY

PATRICIA LAKIN

A BLACKBIRCH PRESS BOOK

WOODBRIDGE, CONNECTICUT

CONTENTS

Published by Blackbirch Press, Inc.
One Bradley Road
Woodbridge, CT 06525

©1995 Blackbirch Press, Inc.
First Edition

10 9 8 7 6 5 4 3 2 1

Photo Credits
Cover: ©Catherine Ursillo/Leo de Wys, Inc.; Series Logo: ©Tanya Stone; p. 3: ©Karen McCunnall/Leo de Wys, Inc.; p. 5: ©Nancy Durrell McKenna/Photo Researchers, Inc.; p. 7: ©Cynthia Brito/DDB Stock Photo; p. 9: ©Jean-Marie Truchet/Tony Stone Worldwide; p. 11: ©Fridmar Damm/Leo de Wys, Inc.; p. 13: ©W. Hille/Leo de Wys, Inc.; p. 15: ©Iraida Icaza/Leo de Wys, Inc.; p. 17: ©Yoram Lehmann/Peter Arnold, Inc.; p. 19: ©Alan Dolgin/Leo de Wys, Inc.; p. 21: ©Tourism Yukon Photo; p. 23: ©Michael Howard/Leo de Wys, Inc.; p. 25: ©Ingeborg Lippman/Peter Arnold, Inc.; p. 27: ©J.B. Grant/Leo de Wys, Inc.; p. 29: ©Blair Seitz/Photo Researchers, Inc.; p. 31: ©Sylvain Grandadam/Photo Researchers, Inc.

Library of Congress Cataloging–in–Publication Data
Lakin, Pat.
    Family / by Patricia Lakin.
        p.   cm.—(We all share)
    Includes bibliographical references and index.
    Summary: Examines the similarities and differences in families around the world.
        ISBN 1-56711-143-2 (lib. bdg.)
        1. Family—Juvenile literature.
    [1. Family.   2. Family life.]
    I. Title.   II. Series.
    HQ518.L25 1995
    306.85—dc20   94-41713
                                              CIP
                                              AC

INTRODUCTION	3
ISRAEL	4
BRAZIL	6
INDIA	8
CHINA	10
RUSSIA	12
PANAMA	14
NIGERIA	16
NATIVE AMERICAN	18
CANADA	20
PORTUGAL	22
IRAQ	24
GREECE	26
UNITED STATES	28
EGYPT	30
GLOSSARY	32
INDEX	32

INTRODUCTION

Families come in all shapes and sizes. Some have two parents. Others have one. Some have grandparents and many other relatives all living together. Others have some families living with other, non-related families.

How each family provides for its members depends on two main things—where the family lives and what resources are available to them.

The goal of families all over the world is basically the same. Whether they live in remote villages or in big cities, families want to make sure their members are fed, clothed, and sheltered. They also hope to teach their children about cultural traditions and family history. This knowledge helps them gain the skills they will need when they become adults.

A Masai family poses for a portrait.

ISRAEL

K*ibbutz* is a Hebrew word that means group. In Israel, a kibbutz is a group of families that lives and works together.

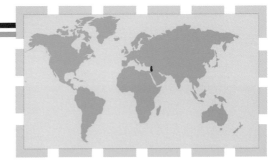

The first kibbutz was started in the early 1900s in the land of Palestine, now known as Israel. Jewish settlers wanted to turn the desert land into fertile fields. They knew their goal would be difficult for individuals to accomplish alone, so they formed a commune, or group, where they could live together and share the work.

Today, Israel has over 300 kibbutz communities. The smallest kibbutz has about 50 people. The largest has over 2,000. Kibbutz families live in their own small houses on the kibbutz grounds. The children go to the kibbutz school. Every adult works either in the fields or in the kibbutz factory. Some may have jobs outside of the kibbutz. Each evening, and on weekends, kibbutz families spend their time together in their own homes or in the kibbutz's recreational facilities. They have the choice of eating meals at home or in the communal dining room. The kibbutz may also offer evening entertainment.

For the three percent of Israeli families who live this way, family time can truly be spent relaxing with one another. That is because many of the routine household chores such as cooking, shopping, and doing laundry are done by other kibbutz workers.

Kids work on the garden in front of one of their kibbutz buildings.

BRAZIL

Brazil is the largest country in South America. Many of Brazil's big cities are located in the southern part of the country.

The products that are grown or produced in the south must be carried to other parts of Brazil or to other countries. Trucks are often used to move goods from one place to another.

In Brazil, many men have jobs as truckers and have to travel a good part of each week. Because many fathers are absent, families usually choose to live close to their relatives. In this way, a Brazilian mother knows that there are many relatives nearby to help with the household chores and child care.

When the men return from their week-long journeys, families spend the weekend relaxing

This Brazilian family lives on the mighty Amazon River near the city of Manaus.

together. When a father is traveling, Brazilian children have their extended family of aunts, uncles, cousins, and grandparents to turn to for care, homework help, or just plain fun!

INDIA

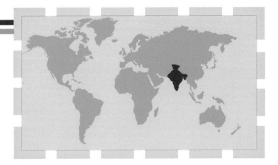

About 800 million people live in the large Asian country of India.

Even though India has several very large cities, the majority of Indians and their families live in small villages. Village life is simple and filled with hard work. The main occupation for a family is to farm the land, or fish if their village is near water.

A rural Indian village may have as many as 200 stone, brick, or mud homes that are built close together. A family traditionally consists of a mother, father, children, married children, uncles, aunts, and grandparents who live in the same village.

Because so many people may be living in small quarters, much family time is spent outside in the courtyard where meals are prepared and eaten. The women of the family are responsible for preparing the food, fetching the water from the well, and

A family in Udaipur stands in their courtyard decorated with a large, colorful mural.

running the household. The men are responsible for working in the fields and tending to the animals. When the young boys and girls are old enough to help, they follow the traditional paths: Girls help their mothers and boys help their fathers.

CHINA

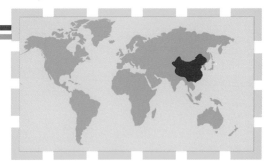

China has the highest population of any country on earth. Because it has so many people, the Chinese government is encouraging married men and women to have only one child. That is why a Chinese child of today may very well have no brothers or sisters.

It is common for a Chinese family to consist of a mother, father, one child, and at least one grandparent. The grandparents in every Chinese family are highly valued members. In China, it is a grandfather who is considered the family's head. He is the ultimate authority figure in the family.

Right: Father and daughter pose for a portrait in one of China's rural provinces.

Chinese grandparents are also the primary caretakers of the family's young children. This is because, in many Chinese families, both the mother and father work outside the home for a six-day work week. Grandmothers in China are also responsible for the day-to-day running of a family household.

RUSSIA

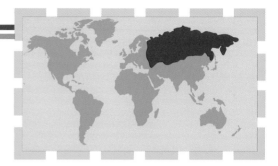

Babushka is the Russian word for a kerchief worn on an older woman's head. That is why many older Russian women are called Babushkas.

Many Babushkas have retired from their jobs and live on pensions, or allowances, from the government. In order to make their small incomes last from one month to the next, Babushkas often move in with a married child and help to run the household.

In most Russian families, both the father and mother work outside of the home. Many important jobs are held by women. In fact, a majority of doctors and engineers in Russia are women.

For these young Russian families, whether they live in rural or urban areas, it is their Babushka who does the important daily chores.

A Russian family gathers together for dinner as the Babushka pours tea.

The Babushka often does the shopping, cooking, cleaning, and caring for the young children. In the evening, the entire family gathers together to enjoy one another's company.

PANAMA

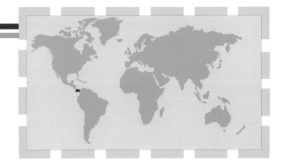

The Republic of Panama is a narrow strip of land called an isthmus. It connects Central America to the continent of South America.

Panama lies between the Atlantic and Pacific oceans. The famous Panama Canal allows ships to travel between the two oceans without having to sail around the entire South American continent. During the early 1900s, many people from other countries were brought to Panama to build the canal. As a result, Panama is a melting pot of cultures. Most of the people live in the country's capital, Panama City. But there are still native Panamanians who live in distant parts of the country. The Choco is one tribe of natives that leads a very simple and work-filled life.

A Choco man is monogamous. That means he will only have one wife. He lives in a patrilineal society. That means the father is the head of the family. When a Choco father dies, everything he owns is inherited by the male family members.

A Choco family lives in a simple house with a cone-shaped roof. Family chores are clearly divided. The men hunt with bows and arrows and spear fish from their *piraguas*, or wooden boats, that they carved from trees. Basket weaving and ceramic making are done by the women. All members of the family, except for young children, work in the fields. As they grow, Choco children are taught by their elders the skills they will eventually need to work and raise their own families.

A grandmother, mother, and daughter from Panama's Kund tribe dress in colorful, handwoven clothes.

NIGERIA

Nigeria is a country on the northwestern coast of Africa. Most Nigerians live in the countryside, in small villages.

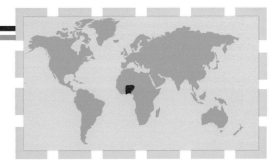

The typical Nigerian family consists of parents, grandparents, aunts, uncles, and cousins all living in the same compound, or group of houses. In this way, everyone from the family shares what they have with one another. Family members help to work the fields, raise the children, prepare the food, and care for the elderly.

The men traditionally go off early in the morning to work in the distant fields. The women most often care for the vegetable gardens and the small animals that are kept at home. When the school and work day end, families have a chance to come together and relax. Most of these villages, however, do not have the

A Nigerian father stands proudly with his two sons in front of their thatched-roof home.

modern forms of entertainment found in Nigerian cities—such as computer games and television. For these families, relaxation means sitting together, talking, and telling stories.

NATIVE AMERICAN

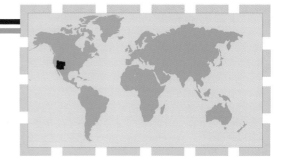

The Navajo—or Diné, as they are also called—are the largest Native American tribe in America today.

Diné, which means "The People," live in all corners of the world. Their ancestral home, however, is located in portions of four neighboring southwestern states in America: Utah, Arizona, New Mexico, and Colorado.

Most of the Diné families who live within this Navajo Nation have kept their ancient family traditions. One of their most important traditions is that of a matrilineal society. That means that the mother and her relatives set the rules. When a young couple marries, for instance, they move in with the wife's clan. Yet, all of the adult members of the family—mother, father, grandparents, aunts, and uncles—help in raising the children.

Everyone in a Diné family is a valued member. The elders are respected because of their experience and wisdom. The children are respected because they will be the ones to carry on the ancient customs and beliefs of the Diné.

A large Navajo clan gathers together for a family portrait.

CANADA

In many ways, this large North American country is similar to its southern neighbor, the United States. Both countries have a large immigrant population and many citizens who have not lived in the country very long.

Many young Canadian adults have moved away from their relatives to seek better jobs in other parts of the giant country.

A Canadian family is primarily a nuclear family. That means it is made up of two parents and their children. The parents are the primary caretakers of their young. If both parents work, they may hire someone to care for their children. Some parents

A family from the Yukon enjoys Canada's great outdoors together.

send their children to a daycare center while they are both at work. In some cases, where there are no relatives living nearby, a Canadian child may develop closer ties with friends and neighbors than with his or her own grandparents, aunts, uncles, and cousins.

PORTUGAL

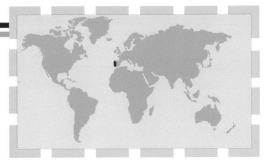

Portugal is a rectangular-shaped country in Europe that is bordered by Spain on the east and the Atlantic Ocean on the west.

In ancient times, Portugal was invaded many times by armies from other countries. The Portuguese tradition called for people to band together to fight off those invaders.

Even though there have not been invasions for hundreds of years, Portuguese families keep their ancient tradition of banding together. They form very strong bonds with all their relatives. In a Portuguese family, when a couple marries, the husband's parents and his extended family members join with the wife's parents and her extended family members. Together, they "adopt" one another and form an even larger family group.

A Portuguese family relaxes as they have lunch on one of their country's beautiful beaches.

IRAQ

Iraq is a Middle Eastern country that is bordered by Iran to the east, Kuwait to the south, and Saudi Arabia to the west. Like its neighbors Saudi Arabia and Iran, most of Iraq's population is Muslim. That means they follow the Islamic religion.

In rural areas, extended family members most likely live together. Iraqi women who live in these areas still wear the traditional robe and veil, or *abaaya*, whenever they go out in public.

The typical urban family in Iraq is a nuclear family. This consists of the parents and their children. Most Iraqi women living in the large cities dress in a more western style and do not wear the *abaaya*.

Throughout Iraq, the family unit is the most important part of an Iraqi's life. If a child is sick or a relative has an emergency, working men or women are automatically given time off from their jobs to take care of their family member.

Iraqi children are secure in knowing there are always many family members watching over their health and well-being.

An Iraqi family enjoys a picnic in a park in Baghdad.

GREECE

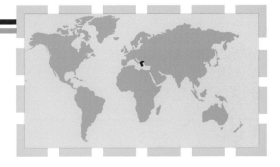

Greece is a small country in Europe that juts out into the Mediterranean Sea. Despite its size, it has a great history. The first European civilization was started in Greece over 2,000 years ago.

Greece's capital, Athens, is home to more than half of the country's population. Greek families who live in or near this city are most often nuclear families. They consist of parents and their children. However, as in most Mediterranean cultures, the extended family—grandparents, aunts, uncles, and cousins—plays a very important role.

In present-day Greece, many women work outside of the home. Because of this, grandparents are often called upon to help care for the family's youngsters.

An extended family in Chios relaxes in the sun outside their stone house.

UNITED STATES

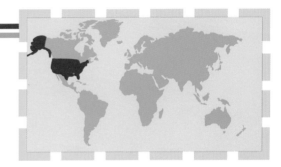

The United States is one of the largest and richest countries in the world. It also has many large cities that are centers for international business.

The nuclear family of two parents and their children used to be the most common in America. Today, however, there are a great many different kinds of families in America, including single-parent families.

For the single-parent family, children most often have their mothers as their primary care giver. If the single mother needs to work, she most often has to find a relative, a friend, or a hired person to care for her children. Daycare is sometimes available for children who are too young to go to school.

In single-parent homes, children may have responsibilities in running the household. While this type of family may not have much time for relaxation, children can develop very strong bonds with their primary parent. As responsible young people, they may learn early the life lessons that help them as adults. President Bill Clinton and the Reverend Jesse Jackson are two of the many successful Americans who are the products of a single-parent home.

A family in Pennsylvania relaxes together in their living room.

EGYPT

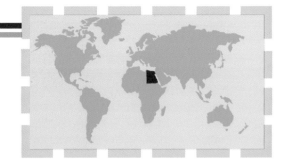

Egypt is located in the northeastern corner of the African continent. It has borders on the Red Sea and the Mediterranean Sea.

More than ninety-six percent of Egypt's people live along the narrow strip of fertile land that surrounds the country's main source of water, the Nile River. A small portion of Egyptians make their homes in the desert areas to the west. Some of the people that live in the desert are nomads. This means they roam from place to place in search of food and water. Most of Egypt's desert-dwellers are called Bedouins.

Many Bedouin families live in mud-brick houses with wooden doors. Bedouin mothers are responsible for sewing the family's clothes and carrying the daily supply of water from a nearby oasis, or watering hole.

A young Egyptian girl takes care of her infant sister.

Many Bedouin fathers spend their days farming the few crops that can grow in the desert, such as oranges, lemons, and olives. Children often receive no formal education. Instead, they help their families survive in the harsh desert environment. Young boys help their fathers with the chores of farming and keeping livestock, such as camels. Young girls help their mothers in their daily routine of providing food and water for the family.

GLOSSARY

ancestral	Relating to one's past relatives or ancestors.
clan	A unit in a tribe or group of people.
commune	A group that lives together and shares equally in the work and profits.
matrilineal	A society in which the mother's line of relatives determines rules and ownership.
monogamous	Having only one husband or wife.
nuclear family	Children and their parents.
patrilineal	A society in which the father's line of relatives determines the rules and ownership.
polygamous	Having more than one husband or wife.
remote	Distant, far off.

INDEX

Abaaya, 24

B*abushka,* 12, 13
Bedouin, 30, 31

Choco, 14, 15
Clinton, Bill, 29

Daycare, 21, 28
Diné. *See* Navajo.
Divorce, 28

Extended family, 7, 22, 26

Grandparents, 7, 8, 10, 11, 16

Jackson, Jesse, 29

K*ibbutz,* 4, 5

Matrilineal family, 18, 19
Muslim, 24, 25

Navajo, 18, 19
Nuclear family, 20, 21, 24, 26, 28

Palestine, 4
Panama Canal, 14
Patrilineal family, 15
Piragua, 15

Single-parent family, 28, 29